What's the Issue?

WHAT'S INCOME INEQUALITY?

By Joseph Stanley

D1418274

KidHaven
PUBLISHING

Published in 2019 by
KidHaven Publishing, an Imprint of Greenhaven Publishing, LLC
353 3rd Avenue
Suite 255
New York, NY 10010

Designer: Andrea Davison-Bartolotta
Editor: Katie Kawa

Photo credits: Cover (top) Constantine Pankin/Shutterstock.com; cover (bottom) Hemera Technologies/AbleStock.com/Thinkstock; p. 5 (right) Crush Rush/Shutterstock.com; p. 5 (left) David Peterlin/Shutterstock.com; p. 6 © iStockphoto.com/TraceRouda; p. 7 creativenv/iStock/Thinkstock; p. 9 a katz/Shutterstock.com; p. 10 360b/Shutterstock.com; p. 11 Ovchinnikova Irina/Shutterstock.com; p. 12 surfertide/iStock/Thinkstock; p. 13 Syda Productions/Shutterstock.com; p. 15 J. Louis Bryson/Shutterstock.com; p. 16 fizkes/iStock/Thinkstock; p. 17 Everett Historical/Shutterstock.com; p. 19 Dan Holm/Shutterstock.com; p. 20 © iStockphoto.com/Steve Debenport; p. 21 (bottom) © iStockphoto.com/Rawpixel; p. 21 (top) tashechka/Shutterstock.com.

Library of Congress Cataloging-in-Publication Data

Names: Stanley, Joseph, author.
Title: What's income inequality? / Joseph Stanley.
Description: First Edition. | New York : KidHaven Publishing, [2019] |
    Series: What's the issue? | Includes index.
Identifiers: LCCN 2018000953 (print) | LCCN 2017060856 (ebook) | ISBN
    9781534525900 (eBook) | ISBN 9781534525870 (library bound book) | ISBN
    9781534525887 (pbk. book) | ISBN 9781534525894 (6 pack)
Subjects: LCSH: Income distribution. | Equality–Social aspects.
Classification: LCC HC79.I5 (print) | LCC HC79.I5 S763 2019 (ebook) | DDC
    339.2/2–dc23
LC record available at https://lccn.loc.gov/2018000953

Printed in the United States of America

CPSIA compliance information: Batch #BS18KL: For further information contact Greenhaven Publishing LLC, New York, New York at 1-844-317-7404.

Please visit our website, www.greenhavenpublishing.com. For a free color catalog of all our high-quality books, call toll free 1-844-317-7404 or fax 1-844-317-7405.

CONTENTS

Not Always Equal

The United States was founded on the belief that "all men are created equal." However, that doesn't mean all people in the United States have been treated equally or given equal opportunities to succeed. Inequality is something Americans are still fighting against today.

One kind of inequality that's talked about often is income inequality. In the United States, there's a big gap between those who make the most money and those who make the least. This means income, or money taken in through work or **investments**, isn't spread out equally among all Americans.

Facing the Facts 🔍

A 2015 report showed that 63 percent of Americans believe the money in their country should be more evenly distributed, or spread out.

Leaders such as President Barack Obama and Senator Bernie Sanders, shown here, have called income inequality one of the biggest problems in the United States today.

Income, Wealth, and Poverty

Some people believe income inequality and poverty are the same thing, but they're different. Poverty is the state of being very poor. Income inequality occurs when there's a big gap between how much money the poor and the rich make. Groups of people are working hard to **solve** these problems.

Income inequality is also different from wealth inequality. Wealth is the total value of properties and things a person or group has. These things include homes, cars, and businesses. Income doesn't include those things.

Facing the Facts 🔍

Wealth inequality in the United States is 10 times worse than income inequality, according to a 2014 study.

Amount of Wealth Held by U.S. Families in Trillions of Dollars

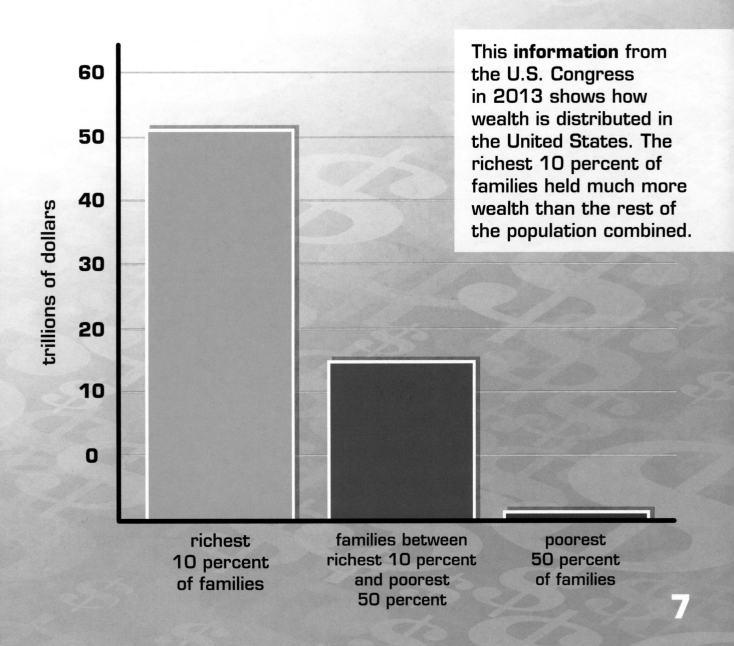

This **information** from the U.S. Congress in 2013 shows how wealth is distributed in the United States. The richest 10 percent of families held much more wealth than the rest of the population combined.

trillions of dollars

60
50
40
30
20
10
0

richest 10 percent of families

families between richest 10 percent and poorest 50 percent

poorest 50 percent of families

By the Numbers

Income inequality can be seen by studying how the total amount of income earned by a group of people is **divided**. In the United States, around half of all the income earned in 2015 went to only the top 10 percent of highest-earning Americans. The other 90 percent of Americans had to share the half that was left.

This large gap between the richest Americans and the rest of the population has gotten worse over time. Some **experts** have stated that income inequality in the 2010s is the highest it's been since the 1920s.

Facing the Facts

A person born in the United States in 1940 had a 92 percent chance of making more money than their parents. Today, a person born in 1980 only has a 50 percent chance of making more money than their parents.

In 2011, a movement called Occupy Wall Street was created to draw attention to income inequality in the United States. People gathered in New York City and in other places around the country to speak out against the growing gap between the very rich, who they called the 1 percent, and the rest of the American people, who they called the 99 percent.

Income Inequality Around the World

Income inequality isn't just a problem in the United States, it's also a problem in other countries. One group that tracks income inequality in different countries is the Organisation for Economic Co-operation and Development (OECD). According to the OECD, income inequality is rising around the world.

As of 2015, Iceland had the lowest level of income inequality of all the countries the OECD tracks. The United States had one of the highest levels of income inequality. The only countries with a higher level of income inequality were Mexico, Chile, and Turkey.

The Gini index is sometimes used to measure income inequality around the world. A Gini index of 0 means all income is shared equally, and a Gini index of 1 means all income is owned by one person.

Iceland, shown here, is one of many countries with a more equal **economy** than the United States, according to the OECD.

Education Is Important

Adults often tell young people that it's important to get a good education. They say this because they believe education is a key to getting a good job and making more money.

The connection between education and income inequality shows that these adults are right. One study found a large gap in incomes between people with only a high school education and people with a **college** education. As of 2015, college **graduates** earned an average of 56 percent more income than people who didn't go to college.

Facing the Facts 🔍

In 1975, 34 percent of jobs required a college education. By 2012, 65 percent of jobs required a college education.

People who graduate from college have a better chance of getting a job and making more money than those who don't go to college. However, not everyone can afford to go to college. Some people believe a college education should be free so that everyone can have equal opportunities.

The Fight for Equal Pay

Income inequality isn't the only kind of inequality in the United States. People are sometimes treated differently because of their race, their sex, or where their families come from. This can **affect** how much money they make.

For example, there's a gap between how much money white Americans make and how much money African Americans and Hispanic Americans make. There's also a gap between how much income men and women earn. As of 2015, the average American woman needed to work an extra 44 days a year to earn the same amount of money as the average American man.

14

Facing the Facts

For every dollar the average white man makes in the United States, white women make 81 cents, black women make 65 cents, and Hispanic women make 59 cents.

Many people in the United States and around the world are working to draw attention to income inequality based on sex, race, and the country a person's family comes from.

OPSEU SEFPO

**SAME WORK?
SAME PAY.**

collegefaculty.org

OPSEU SEFPO

BETTER

We work for

The Great Recession

Income inequality can also be affected by major economic events. In 2007, the U.S. economy began to **decline**. This period of economic problems became known as the Great Recession, and it lasted until 2009. During this time, economic activity slowed down and the number of people without jobs—also known as the unemployment rate—grew.

The Great Recession affected all Americans—from the very rich to the very poor. However, the very rich took less time than other Americans to **recover** from the recession. This created more of a gap between the very rich and everyone else.

Facing the Facts

Four months after the end of the Great Recession, the unemployment rate reached a high of 10 percent. This means that 10 percent of the people in the United States who could work didn't have a job.

JOB SEARCH

Log in

ND JOB

The Great Recession has been called the worst period of economic problems since the Great Depression of the 1930s.

Fixing the Problem

People have many different ideas about how to solve the problem of income inequality. Some people believe creating more jobs for people without a college education will help. Others are working to create training programs for those who need work or want better-paying jobs.

Raising the minimum wage is another plan some people have to help the lowest-paid workers in the United States. The minimum wage is the lowest amount a worker can be paid. People who support raising the minimum wage believe no one who works a full-time job should be living in poverty.

Facing the Facts 🔍

In a 2017 report, 74 percent of Americans said they supported raising the minimum wage.

Some people strongly support raising the minimum wage. Others believe it could hurt businesses that can't afford to pay people more and could cause the prices of many goods to go up.

Ways to Help

Income inequality is a part of life in the United States, and people explain why it exists it in different ways. Some people believe the richest people work harder than anyone else, while others believe they got rich because they had more advantages. In the same way, some people believe those who are poor don't work hard enough, while others believe people live in poverty because of things they can't control.

Income inequality is a big problem. However, everyone can do their part to make sure people are treated fairly—no matter how much money they have.

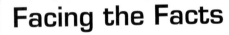

Facing the Facts

A 2014 study showed that more than half of Americans believed the government should play some part in closing the gap between the rich and everyone else.

WHAT CAN **YOU** DO?

Learn more about the causes and effects of income inequality.

Raise money or spend time working with a group that helps the poor.

Learn more about plans to fight all kinds of inequality and leaders who support those plans.

Treat everyone with respect, and don't let how much money a person has affect how you treat them.

How can you help make the world a more equal place? These are just a few ideas to help you get started!

GLOSSARY

affect: To produce an effect on something.

college: A school people can go to after high school.

decline: To become worse or weaker.

divide: To split among different groups.

economy: The way in which goods and services are made, sold, and used in a country or area.

expert: Someone who has a special skill or knowledge.

graduate: A person who has finished the required course of study in a school. Also, to finish a course of study in a school.

information: Facts about something.

investment: Money put out to gain more money in return.

recover: To get back to the way things were before.

solve: To find an answer or a way to deal with a problem.

FOR MORE INFORMATION

WEBSITES

Be a Volunteer

kidshealth.org/en/kids/volunteering.html

Volunteering is a good way to help those who are struggling with income inequality and poverty, and this website provides tips on how to volunteer.

Economy for Kids

www.scholastic.com/browse/collection.jsp?id=455

This collection of activities and articles helps explain economic issues.

BOOKS

Hollander, Barbara Gottfried. *What Are Saving and Spending?* New York, NY: Britannica Educational Publishing, 2017.

Kenney, Karen Latchana, and Steve Stankiewicz. *Economics Through Infographics.* Minneapolis, MN: Lerner Publications Company, 2015.

Riggs, Kate. *The Great Recession.* Mankato, MN: Creative Education, 2017.

INDEX